THIS IS ME! 2022

MY VOICE IN VERSE

Edited By Byron Tobolik

First published in Great Britain in 2022 by:

YoungWriters Est. 1991

Young Writers
Remus House
Coltsfoot Drive
Peterborough
PE2 9BF
Telephone: 01733 890066
Website: www.youngwriters.co.uk

All Rights Reserved
Book Design by Ashley Janson
© Copyright Contributors -0001
Softback ISBN 978-1-80459-249-6

Printed and bound in the UK by BookPrintingUK
Website: www.bookprintinguk.com
YB0MA0008A

FOREWORD

For Young Writers' latest competition This Is Me, we asked primary school pupils to look inside themselves, to think about what makes them unique, and then write a poem about it! They rose to the challenge magnificently and the result is this fantastic collection of poems in a variety of poetic styles.

Here at Young Writers our aim is to encourage creativity in children and to inspire a love of the written word, so it's great to get such an amazing response, with some absolutely fantastic poems. It's important for children to focus on and celebrate themselves and this competition allowed them to write freely and honestly, celebrating what makes them great, expressing their hopes and fears, or simply writing about their favourite things. This Is Me gave them the power of words. The result is a collection of inspirational and moving poems that also showcase their creativity and writing ability.

I'd like to congratulate all the young poets in this anthology, I hope this inspires them to continue with their creative writing.

CONTENTS

Independent Entries

Michael Baldwin	1
Aaliya Skinner (9)	2

Abbey Primary School, Newtownards

Samuel Poole (9)	3
Lucy Dallimer (8)	4
Jessica Bunting (8)	5
Rubi Massey (8)	6

Al-Huda Primary School, Bolton

Abdul Hayy Atcha (9)	7
Huzefa Shah (10)	8

Ashfield Junior School, Bushey

Raiden Kotecha (8)	9
Rowan Welsby (7)	10
Adam Hearn (8)	11

Aylward Primary School, Stanmore

Zarina Bakhtani (9)	12
Antonia Nathan-Laville (10)	13
Lordina Asante Kyeremeh (11)	14
Luca Hutanu (10)	15
Diva Mehta (9)	16
Khajurei Raseharan (9)	17

Bailiffe Bridge Junior & Infant School, Bailiffe Bridge

Jack Griffiths (9)	18

Ballymagee Primary School, Bangor

Ivy Lumsden (8)	19

Ballysally Primary School, Ballysally

Scott Lindsay (10)	20

Balmuildy Primary School, Bishopbriggs

Eilidh Armstrong (9)	21
Fraser Dick (8)	22
Cole Robinson (9)	23
Alfie Keith (9)	24
Finlay Paker (9)	25

Barmby Moor CE Primary School, Barmby Moor

Madalin Farrow (11)	26

Bearbrook Combined School, Aylesbury

Joseph Kneller (7)	27
Areeda Nisar (8)	28
Maisie Hughes (8)	29
Oscar Raamesh (8)	30

Bearsden Primary School, Bearsden

Lucy Oliver (10)	31
Isla Clark (10)	32

Belswains Primary School, Hemel Hempstead

Ava Loughney (9)	33

Blairhall Primary School, Blairhall

William Rodger (10)	34
Sophie Rowley (9)	35

Blakehill Primary School, Idle

Lacey Ansbro (9)	36

Brighton Avenue Primary School, Gateshead

Mya Johnson (8)	37
Grace Thompson (8)	38
Callum Cook (8)	39

Bunscoil Cholmcille, Derry City

PJ Watson (8)	40
Cathaoir Doherty (8)	41
Eadaoin Doherty (8)	42
Maeve Meehan (7)	43

Calveley Primary Academy, Calveley

Jamie Smyth	44

Castle Academy, Northampton

King Ekele (9)	45
Aubrey Thomson (9)	46
Ayobami Alabi (9)	47

Cawood CE Primary School, Cawood

Joshua Bucknall (10)	48
Ella Craven (10)	49
Harry Carrier (10)	50

Collingbourne CE Primary School, Marlborough

Matilda Emily North (9)	51

Cradle Hill Community Primary School, Seaford

Luke	52

Cromer Junior School, Cromer

Chester Bayes (8)	53
Ronnie Chatten (8)	54

Didcot Primary Academy, Great Western Park

Lilly Holt (10)	55
Sumaiya Fatima (10)	56

East Sheen Primary School, London

Toni Arts (8)	57

Eastbury Community School, Barking

Amaar Rahman (11)	58

Goddard Park Community Primary School, Swindon

Jasmine (11)	59
Chukwuemeka John (11)	60
Coco Yarahmadi (11)	61

Hampton Hargate Primary School, Hampton Hargate

Niamh Woodley (8)	62
Midun Odenusi (9)	63
Chizara Idika (9)	64
Charlie Jackson (9)	65
Teniola Ojo (9)	66
Ethan Fomoriys (9)	67
Layden-Ray Beebe (9)	68
Rafael Sorace Rocha (9)	69

Harris Primary Academy Mayflower, Chafford Hundred

Poppy Przybyszewski (8)	70

Heriot Primary School, Heriot

Benjamin Wallace (10)	71
Archie James Mieduniecki (9)	72
Katie Robertson (10)	73

High Mill Primary School, Carluke

Maya Bennie (8)	74
Kylah Hunter (8)	75

Hob Moor Primary Academy, Acomb

Rian Gibson (10)	76
Dylan Lambert (10)	78
Ella Price-Bestford	79

Holy Child Primary School, Creggan Estate

Hallie Wrench (10)	80

Holy Family Primary School, Downpatrick

Hannah Morrissey	81

Holy Rosary & St Anne's Catholic Primary School, Leeds

Aiden Moyo (9)	82

Ilfracombe CE Junior School, Ilfracombe

Maddie Young (9)	83
Kolby Owen (9)	84
Leo Dainty (8)	85

International School Of Gabon Ecole Ruban Vert, Gabon

Codaccioni Paule (11)	86
Francesca Sernia (11)	87

Irish Society's Primary School, Coleraine

Sienna McConnell-Elliott (9)	88
Ben Linton (9)	89

ISML Primary (International School Michel Lucius), Luxembourg

James Ezekiel Andrews (9)	90

Jessop Primary School, Herne Hill

Yassin Serroukh (8)	91

Kilgraston School, Bridge Of Earn

Daisy Daly	92

Kintore Primary School, Kintore

Nathan Pritchard (11) — 93

Kirkcaldy West Primary School, Kirkcaldy

Evan Ness (12)	94
Benjamin Clayton (11)	95
Abderrahmane Braham Chaouch (11)	96
Millie June Ovens (11)	97
Ethan Learmonth (11)	98

Logie Primary School, Dunphail

Teddy Gadalla — 99

Loreburn Primary School, Dumfries

Stanlie Leslie (9) — 100

Loretto Junior School, Musselburgh

Jake Gray (11) — 101

Manston Primary School, Crossgates

Jak Donnison (11)	103
Lily Turner (10)	104
Sophie May Croft (11)	105
Lewis Clayton (10)	106

Marshfield Primary School, Little Horton

Aroosh Haider	107
Hafsah-Aiman Younas (8)	108
Amima Butt (8)	110
Hajirah Hussain (8)	111
Azaan Ahmed (9)	112

Model Church In Wales Primary School, Carmarthen

Grace Beer (8)	113
Dihansa Dewsiluni Manamperi (8)	114
Isabel Otterburn (9)	115

Motcombe CE VA Primary School, Shaftesbury

Lucas-Eli Hargrave (9)	116
Thomas Richens (9)	117
Summer Robertson (9)	118

North Hinksey CE Primary School, North Hinksey

Betsy Billings (9)	119
Amelia Wing (9)	120

Northcote Primary School, Liverpool

Emily McGimpsey (11) — 121

Oasis Academy Marksbury Road, Bristol

Reuben Wright (7)	122
Oscar Watkins (6)	123
Jelani Ricketts (6)	124
Lorenzo Sutera (7)	125
Klay Walton (7)	126
Abdilatif Abiib (7)	127
Tommy Singleton (6)	128
Gabriel Magro (7)	129
Lily Fletcher-Wilmut (6)	130
Jacoby Cunningham (7)	131
Leyland Chard (7)	132
Imogen Tinline (7)	133
Esme Forsyth (6)	134
Taihir Medley-Hutchins (7)	135
Joey Parsons (6)	136
Oliver Morgan (7)	137

Ariana Timinskaite (7)	138
Sylvie Frazier-Brown (7)	139
Sophia Smith (7)	140

Park Community School, Leigh Park

Isabella Angell (12)	141
Joshua Musasa	142

Park School For Girls, Ilford

Shivam Solanki (8)	143

Parkwood Primary School, Keighley

Thomas Mac Lockley (8)	144

Ponsbourne St Mary's CE Primary School, Hertford

Berri-Rae Pryor (8)	145
Ava Sims (8)	146

Radford Academy, Radford

Waslat Saberi (8)	147

Rosedale Primary School, Hayes

Mominah Mohammed (9)	148
Saina Langani (10)	149
Sachleen Kaur (10)	150
Ahmed Ali Shahid (10)	151

Rosehill School, Nottingham

Harmilton O Agbota Okungbor (14)	152

Saint Xavier Nursery And Primary School, India

Dhanvanthkrishnan Saravanan (7)	153

Salisbury Manor Primary School, Chingford

Renee Appiah-Kubi (10)	154

Sandown Primary School, Deal

Layla West (9)	155
Eden Cope-Lamb (9)	156
Rae Young (9)	157
Daisy Todd (9)	158
Charlie James Reid (9)	159
Finley Lawson (9)	160

South Wootton Junior School, South Wootton

Henry Rudd (10)	161
Arthur Calton (9)	162
Caleb W (11)	163
Eli Ssekabuzza (9)	164

Springfield Primary School, Rowley Regis

Eva Ansley (8)	165
Eliza Bates (9)	166

St Benedict's Catholic Primary School, Hindley

Vanessa Disley (7)	167

St Bride's Primary School, Bothwell

Yousaf Ali (8)	168
Chloe Meikle (8)	169
Stella McCluskey (8)	170

St Bridget's Primary RC School, Baillieston

Tariq Lwanyaga (11) — 171

St Columb's Primary School Cullion, Desertmartin

Molly-Kate O'Connor (11) — 172

St Helen's RC Primary School, Brixton

Richard Bykowski (9) — 173
Jaydan B (9) — 174

St Ignatius Catholic Primary School, Ossett

Amelie R (10) — 175
Niamh N (10) — 176
Mason Cusworth (9) — 177

St Margaret's CE Junior School, Rainham

Kavya Panchal (9) — 178

St Mary's Primary School, Maghery

Ceallaigh McCrory (8) — 179
Dylan Convie (11) — 180

St Mary's RC Primary School, Swinton

Nadia Alichniewicz (10) — 181
Phoebe Gore (10) — 182
Jake Braphy (10) — 183
Freya Darby (10) — 184

St Patrick's Catholic Primary School, Birmingham

Emilia Kozlowska (9) — 185

St Patrick's Primary School, Hilltown

Madeline Bye (10) — 186
Emily Read (10) — 188
Ellie Mae McGinn (10) — 189
Seamus Barber (10) — 190
Niamh Farrell (10) — 191
Darragh Harrison (10) — 192

St Peter's CE First School, Marchington

Olivia Ball (8) — 193

St Winefride's Primary School, Manor Park

Cairo Irons (11) — 194

Stanton Drew Primary School, Stanton Drew

Bonny Clutterbuck (11) — 195

Summerfield Primary School, Leeds

Maya Milner (11) — 198
Jennifer Beaumont (8) — 199

Sutton High Prep School, Sutton

Manahil Zaidi (9) — 200

Sutton-on-Trent Primary & Nursery School, Sutton-On-Trent

Summer Ballard (9)	201

The Ferncumbe CE Primary School, Hatton

Isabella Brookfield (8)	202

Towers Junior School, Hornchurch

George Johnson (10)	203

Upton Priory School, Macclesfield

Kayden Houghton (9)	204

Victoria Park Primary Academy, Smethwick

Aisha Drammeh (9)	205

Warden Hill Primary School, Warden Hill

Molly Jones	206

Widey Court Primary School, Crownhill

Kacy Welch (11)	207

Worsbrough Common Primary School, Worsbrough Common

Antoni Panasewicz (9)	208
Amelia Rose (8)	209
Ayan Nakoul (8)	210
Phoebe Lunn (9)	211
Libbie Storey (9)	212

THE POEMS

All About Me!

M y favourite animal is a monkey, as soft as a blanket.
I have many favourite, fantastic foods which are sandwiches, burgers, pasta.
C hoosing my favourite games, they are Gorilla Tag and Minecraft Dungeons.
H aving friends, I have Johannes, Jake, Cosmo, Freddie, Jack, Dean and Arman.
A nd a game me and my friends are making is called Chickenopia, which is as cool as being in a UFO.
E ven though I'm not the best artist, I still enjoy drawing daft doodles.
L oving winter, I always enjoy playing in the snow that's as soft as a fluffy cloud.

Michael Baldwin

This Is Me

A for amazing,
S for smart,
C for cute.

Hi, I'm nice to you,
I am silly sometimes,
You are loving.

This is me.

Aaliya Skinner (9)

All About Me

My name is Samuel Harrison Poole
I am not anybody's fool
When at school I read and write
I like my friends and I won't fight
At home I like to work and play
I study the planets every day
My favourite planet is called Saturn
Rings around it make it a lovely pattern
My favourite subject is mathematics
My grandad gave me a book from his attic
Multiplying the numbers makes them bigger
Sometimes it's hard to make them figure.

Samuel Poole (9)
Abbey Primary School, Newtownards

Me, Myself And I

Hi, my name is Lucy
And I'm five plus three
It's not my favourite subject
But mathematics is key
I go to Abbey Primary
And I'm in P4
Miss Craig is my teacher
And her name's on the door
I listen in class
And have fun with my friends
Because in my wee school
The fun never ends
I have lots of hobbies
My favourite one is dance
I can jump around
Like there's ants in my pants.

Lucy Dallimer (8)
Abbey Primary School, Newtownards

All Of Me

J oyful and jolly
E verybody's friend
S uper awesome
S uper smart
I ntelligent and cool
C rafty and fun
A wesome at martial arts.

Jessica Bunting (8)
Abbey Primary School, Newtownards

Enzo The Pup

Enzo is my pup
He is very bitey
But cute
He runs fast
Faster than an aeroplane
He gives the best kisses
That's why I love him the best!

Rubi Massey (8)
Abbey Primary School, Newtownards

The Companions I Admire

Companion of the cave.
Buried next to a special grave.
The one with two lights.
The one who slept on the messenger's bed on one of the nights.
A living martyr.
Wife was Asma, mother was Saffiya.
Half his wealth in charity he gave,
The one who saw paradise beautified for him before he was placed in his grave.
When he was 17, he accepted Islam upon which his mother kept a strike for hunger.
He broke his teeth whilst removing a chain despite feeling so much pain.
He hid Islam from his brother-in-law,
Who came to the companion's house and was shocked by what he saw.
Who are these companions?
The ones who were given the glad tidings of paradise from the Prophet (S.A.W).

Abdul Hayy Atcha (9)
Al-Huda Primary School, Bolton

Huzefa Shah

Huzefa met a flagon dragon at a lair,
Huzefa, Huzefa didn't care,

The dragon was hungry,
The dragon was chunky,
The dragon said, "Mr, how do you do?
Now I'll eat you!"

Huzefa, Huzefa didn't worry,
Huzefa didn't scream or scurry.

He got his gloves,
And burned the dragon,
With *wongan flagon bom.*

Huzefa Shah (10)
Al-Huda Primary School, Bolton

Raiden

R ad as Romero
A nd I don't like scarecrows
I n my house is my football
D on't think my friends don't play hardball
E veryone calls me Raid
N ot by my real name.

Raiden Kotecha (8)
Ashfield Junior School, Bushey

Rowan's Ingredients Poem

A pinch of happiness,
A slab of maths,
A chunk of silliness,
A sprinkle of speed,
This is what you'll have to combine to get me.

Rowan Welsby (7)
Ashfield Junior School, Bushey

Adam

A bit of mischief,
A lot of sugar,
A drop of lemon,
A spoonful of fun,
A sniff of flowers,
A lot of love,
This is me.

Adam Hearn (8)
Ashfield Junior School, Bushey

All Of Me

This is a poem that's all about me
From the top of my head to the soles of my feet
I'm funny, I'm happy, I'm helpful, I'm kind
I've no favourite colour, I can't make up my mind
I really love school, my teachers, my friends
I like reading stories, right up to the end
I'm sporty, I'm friendly, I'm cheerful, I'm glad
I love painting pictures on my great art pad
I'd eat pizza all day, I just wouldn't stop
Or big ripe juicy strawberries with ice cream on top
I'm silly, I'm jolly, I'm tickly, I'm wise
I'm off to eat cheeseburgers and curly French fries
Or should I eat a pie?

Zarina Bakhtani (9)
Aylward Primary School, Stanmore

Me

I'm a mixed-raced girl,
In a whirl of a world.
I have curly hair and deep brown eyes.
The skies so blue, I wish you knew,
how people put on a disguise in front of my eye.
I see they're unhappy and give them a smile.
I'd give them a hug and hug for a while.
I'll say, "Look at me and give me a smile,
it looks beautiful" and we will smile for a while.
I'm not just like the other kids,
who think it's fairy tales.
I learn from mistakes, 'cause everybody fails.
I try to do the best I can
So I'll never need any type of wealthy man.
And that is all now.

Antonia Nathan-Laville (10)
Aylward Primary School, Stanmore

This Is Me

I've got dark eyes
The colour of luscious flies
I've got dark black hair
I'd say the length is pretty fair

I am very clueless
And prefer to walk around shoeless
I write a lot
Although my stories end with an odd plot

I'd preferably watch movies
I have a weird obsession with smoothies
I really love snow
And from this point on
That's all you'd have to know.

Lordina Asante Kyeremeh (11)
Aylward Primary School, Stanmore

My Brain Machine

This is my brain
My brain cycles of laughter
My brain gets mind blown by YouTube
My brain sees a ghost
Like brave, beautiful Macbeth

My brain fights off lies
My brain hugs a teddy when sleeping
My brain makes a boom, crash sound
My brain plays Roblox and video games

My brain wears elegant clothes
My br...
Argh!
My brain has a jumpscare of a fright!

Luca Hutanu (10)
Aylward Primary School, Stanmore

In My Head I Have...

In my head, I have...

99% smartness
But not that good with artiness

I have 100% creativity
I work to the best of my ability

I have eyes like a hawk
And I am quite good with talk

I am truly kind
Both physically and in my mind

But what else do I have in my head?

Diva Mehta (9)
Aylward Primary School, Stanmore

If Only...

My sun, my moon, my stars
The thundering storm
That calls for afar

My evening, my morning
My brand-new day
The gentle wind
That has blown away

And I sang
As I danced in the
Moment I saw you...

If only you had noticed.

Khajurei Raseharan (9)
Aylward Primary School, Stanmore

This Is Me!

My name is Jack G
My favourite fruit is an apple, my favourite colour is red
I like football, it's my favourite sport
I like maths, my pet is called Evie
And she is a cat and a girl
I live in England, I go to Bailiffe Bridge Primary School
I support Liverpool
I love fruits and veg
Coming to school to learn new things
My eye colour is blue, I help people if they need help
I have good ears!

Jack Griffiths (9)
Bailiffe Bridge Junior & Infant School, Bailiffe Bridge

I Am Ivy

I am Ivy and I'm very kind

A lover of nature is me right here
M ajor imagination and very talented

I am the best place to go if you want to draw cartoons
V ery busy like a bee but as fast as a cheetah
Y ay, yay! Hip, hip, hooray for me, Ivy!

Ivy Lumsden (8)
Ballymagee Primary School, Bangor

Rap Star

This is me
Right, I'm going to start slow
So here it goes, ding do!
Enough of that
I'm about, let's start from head to toe
You ready? Here goes
My mind's like a machine
I like KFC
I think music is key
But hey, I'm pretty funny
Wait? Your nose is runny!
I can do maths like 1, 2, 3
It's not hard really, or is it?
Anyway, I've got some skills
Thank goodness I don't pay the bills!
I'm kind sometimes
I can make my teeth grind
But whatever, it's fine
Do you want a dime?
I'm brave enough but I'll be frightened
If I got hit by a massive truck!

Scott Lindsay (10)
Ballysally Primary School, Ballysally

This Is Me

T hankful in my own way
H appy most days
I nterested in a nosy way
S ociable, I love talking too much

I deas, ideas, ideas and more
S mart, my brain works very fast

M indful, I respect others' choices
E ilidh - me in all of these ways.

Eilidh Armstrong (9)
Balmuildy Primary School, Bishopbriggs

This Is Me

F ortnite is my favourite game
R unning is fun
A pples are tasty
S witch is my favourite device
E aster is amazing
R eally love wraps, they're my favourite lunch food.

Fraser Dick (8)
Balmuildy Primary School, Bishopbriggs

This Is Me

    C   ool as a pool
    O   riginal
    L   istens
    E   xcited for the holidays

I love football
My ball is a bouncy ball but bigger

I like Minecraft and Roblox.

Cole Robinson (9)
Balmuildy Primary School, Bishopbriggs

This Is Me

A pples, I like the smoothness.
L ying down I feel relaxed.
F ortnite I like to play with my friends.
I like playing with my friends.
E asy work is fun to do.

Alfie Keith (9)
Balmuildy Primary School, Bishopbriggs

This Is Me

My name is Finlay
And I like cats and dogs.
I like frogs and I like sloths
And I like moths.
I like rocks and I like Fortnite
And my cat purring all night.

Finlay Paker (9)
Balmuildy Primary School, Bishopbriggs

Travelling Lass

M adalin Olivea Farrow I am
A untie and sister, we are a big clan
D riving the wagons
A nd moving our camps
L iving the life of a travelling lass
I n lay-bys and fields while our horses graze
N ever know where we're going the following days

F riends we make along the way
A ttending schools then going away
R eading and writing we do but try
R aising our family we just get by
O ur life is different I will admit but
W e wouldn't change it for one little bit.

Madalin Farrow (11)
Barmby Moor CE Primary School, Barmby Moor

My Favourite Animal

I'm a creature of the sea
There's barnacles covering me
I move slowly but never fast
I don't bother about rafts
I have a loud call which wakes creatures from their bed
I am as grey as lead.
What am I?

Answer: A whale.

Joseph Kneller (7)
Bearbrook Combined School, Aylesbury

This Is Me

I like flowers
I love hanging out with my friends
I love my family
I love playing Roblox

I am a kind, caring and a calm person
I am short like a mouse
I am proud to be me
You should too!

Areeda Nisar (8)
Bearbrook Combined School, Aylesbury

Person I Love

He kisses me goodnight
Sleeps every morning
Loves sweets and me
Likes football
Supports Arsenal
Watches his phone
He likes dogs.
Who is he?

Answer: My stepdad.

Maisie Hughes (8)
Bearbrook Combined School, Aylesbury

What Am I?

I live in a jungle
I am as loud as a plane
I have a lot of black stripes
I surprise my prey and eat them every day
What am I?

Answer: I am a tiger.

Oscar Raamesh (8)
Bearbrook Combined School, Aylesbury

Lucy Is Amazing

L oud
U nicorn lover
C reative with art
Y appy

O lives are really good
L ovely at art
I love to swim
V ulnerable
E xcellent at everything
R ainbow imagination.

Lucy Oliver (10)
Bearsden Primary School, Bearsden

This Is Me

This is me, Isla
I am ten years old
I like to use clay moulds
I am a sister of two
It's very nice to meet you

This is not the end
I hope we can be friends
I enjoy sport
And I am not short

This is me, Isla.

Isla Clark (10)
Bearsden Primary School, Bearsden

This Is Me

T he class that I have is amazing.
H aving lots of cousins is great.
I have two sisters.
S ummer is my favourite season.

I love my friends and family.
S weets are one of my favourite foods.

M illy is my best friend.
E ating ice cream is the best.

Ava Loughney (9)
Belswains Primary School, Hemel Hempstead

Tom And Jerry

T om, the athletic, goofy cat
O bstacle jumping Spike and Tyke
M ischievous, sneaky, creepy crawling mice

A hilarious, crazy, silly cartoon
N ever ever stop fighting each other and
D on't disturb Spike!

J erry, the menace of a mouse
E xasperating cats and dogs
R unning, sleek mouse
R apidly chased around the house
Y anking Tom about the city.

William Rodger (10)
Blairhall Primary School, Blairhall

Sophie

S uch nice eyes
O utstanding hair
P hones are my life
H air is life because
I t is nice
E ducation makes me smart.

Sophie Rowley (9)
Blairhall Primary School, Blairhall

All About Me!

Hi, I'm Lacey and I love dance, school and reading.
I love school because I learn lots and see my friends.
I am a big sister to my brother Charlie and I have a big sister called Maddie.
I love board games like Monopoly and Frustration.
I go to dance on Monday, Wednesday, Friday and Saturday.
I love dance and I think I am good.
I love going on holiday with my family.
I love my birthday, I can't wait because my birthday is on Easter Day.
I love drawing at home and writing stories.
I love doing face masks for my family and stuff like that.

Lacey Ansbro (9)
Blakehill Primary School, Idle

This Is Me

I am Mya
The daughter of Karl and Ashley
Who loves games
Who hates spiders
Who admires my mam
Who fears the dark
Who dreams of karate
Who needs my mum and dad
Pupil of Brighton Avenue
Resident of Gateshead
I am Mya.

Mya Johnson (8)
Brighton Avenue Primary School, Gateshead

About Me

I am Grace
Daughter of Angela and Stuart
Who loves dogs
Who hates teeth
Who admires Jasmine
Who fears lifts
Who dreams of dogs
Who needs sleep
Pupil of Year 3
A resident of the UK
I am Grace.

Grace Thompson (8)
Brighton Avenue Primary School, Gateshead

My Feelings

My happiness is red like a rose
My anger is black as the dark
My love is pink like candyfloss
My kindness is blue like the sky
My caring is yellow like the sun.

Callum Cook (8)
Brighton Avenue Primary School, Gateshead

This Is Me

I am a super striker,
When they see me coming they chase me down.
They're too slow.
They can't catch up because I am too fast
In my lightning bolt boots.
I am good in them and I am a good keeper.
No one can score because...
I
Am
A
Beast!

PJ Watson (8)
Bunscoil Cholmcille, Derry City

This Is Me

   C ome to school
   A lways gaming
   T op hurler
   H ome is my favourite
   A t the toyshop
   O range is my favourite colour
   I love my look
a **R** e you my friend?

Cathaoir Doherty (8)
Bunscoil Cholmcille, Derry City

This Is Me

E ats chocolate.
A magic door.
D ogs are my favourite.
A mazing friends.
O range is my favourite fruit.
I love my friends.
N o carrots eaten!

Eadaoin Doherty (8)
Bunscoil Cholmcille, Derry City

This Is Me

M agic milk.
A magic door.
E xtra dinner.
V ery funny.
E specially at school.

Maeve Meehan (7)
Bunscoil Cholmcille, Derry City

What I Like...

I like...
Diving dogs
Tasty chewy chocolate
Lovely Lego sets
Likeable Lego characters
Fantastic friends
Delightful dreams
Incredible imagination
My funny family
And lastly... me!

Jamie Smyth
Calveley Primary Academy, Calveley

A Glimpse Of Me

He is called the king of his domain.
He isn't as big as the elephant, he thinks he is.
He isn't as fast as a cheetah, he thinks he is.
He isn't as tall as the giraffe, he thinks he is.
He isn't as strong as the hippopotamus, he thinks he is.
His mindset and attitude make him think so, he is unique.

He's as cool as a cucumber, yet can be as busy as a bee.
When cold as ice an interesting story could light up a smile.
He dreams day and night, passionate about football.
Desiring to be as swift as a deer, just like the greatest footballer and goal scorer of our time.

One thing he believes, like the vision of an eagle, his dreams come clear for he knows that a good attitude and the right mindset will get him all he dreams of.

King Ekele (9)
Castle Academy, Northampton

I Am Me

I am me

A mazing as can be
M aybe sometimes annoying

M any people are annoying, don't blame me
E very day working hard, that is me.

Aubrey Thomson (9)
Castle Academy, Northampton

Be Kind

You are strong and brave,
Spread kindness to people that are down.
Inspire people by singing out loud
So don't you quit as you are spreading kind words.

Ayobami Alabi (9)
Castle Academy, Northampton

Football

I come home!
I play football, I kick the ball, it sounds like a bomb!
I practise, practise, practise!
My brother comes, he shoots, I save, save, save!
I shoot, shoot, shoot, my brother does not save!

We play again!
I miss, miss, miss!
He scores, scores, scores!
My brother tries to save my shot but cannot get there!
He shoots, it hits the crossbar, I score.

Joshua Bucknall (10)
Cawood CE Primary School, Cawood

This Poem Is All About Me

Hello, my name is Ella and I'm ten years old
I'm ginger and I'm a ninja
My eyes are emerald-green like trees' leaves
I have the best family in the world.

I love to dance, sing and prance
My favourite country is France
My favourite colour is blue
If you didn't know that about me too.

Ella Craven (10)
Cawood CE Primary School, Cawood

Myself

I am ten years old and I like football.
I have a dog called Louie.
I like watching TV and playing on my PlayStation.
I like running, biking and playing basketball.
I go to the park with my friends and play football.

Harry Carrier (10)
Cawood CE Primary School, Cawood

Confident Or Shy?

I'm pretty shy,
So don't tell me,
I could be an actress,
Just imagine,
I can't even raise my voice,
It's simply untrue that,
I could face an audience,
Because
I'm pretty shy,
And it's a lie to say
I could be an actress.

(Now read it from the bottom)

I'm very confident.

Matilda Emily North (9)
Collingbourne CE Primary School, Marlborough

This Is Me

This is a poem,
A poem about me,
About things that I like,
And who I wanna be.
In this case a footballer,
One that's bold,
And then go help people,
I like warm, but not cold,
I like to talk,
Like, way too much,
I know about things,
Like the Spanish and the Dutch.
But, sadly, my time has run out,
But win me this thing,
And don't make me count!

Luke
Cradle Hill Community Primary School, Seaford

This Is Me

You might find me outside playing football,
You might find me in my house,
You might find me in my bed,
You might find me playing my Switch on the sofa,
You might find me watching TV while in my cover,
You might find me sleeping while beneath me, my sister is snoring,
You might find me in my dad's house.

Chester Bayes (8)
Cromer Junior School, Cromer

This Is Me

You might find me on the iPad under the blanket.
You might find me outside feeling my rabbit.
You might find me in my room a lot.
You might find me downstairs reading.
You might find me behind my bed.
You might find me outside playing football.
You might find me in my living room playing FIFA 22.

Ronnie Chatten (8)
Cromer Junior School, Cromer

Lilly Is Her Name

L ovely, loud, like a tree, what else can describe me?
I look at the wind and watch the breeze in the field
L ike a flower that I desire, it's called a lily and look
L illy, that's my name
Y ellow sun, green trees and our loyal bees

I watch down, without a frown
S he stares at me and I smile

H ens, sheep, cows, pigs, farming is an amazing sight
E nglish, maths, then lunch break
R outine for my school day

N ever angry just my smile, just like the sun
A nimals are so cute (but not ones that bite)
M inecraft and Roblox are my favourite games
E verything is amazing but this is me.

Lilly Holt (10)
Didcot Primary Academy, Great Western Park

Each Raindrop Is A Metaphor

R ow your dreams and destinies
A far.
I will sit on a lonely shore,
N ow mending my nets and sighing.
D awn out, far to sea, a dolphin herd.
R un for the love song she was singing,
O h, she swam like an arrow, straight and true,
P lease, my friend, sit beside me!

A nd out of the sea did she run, with hair black as coal,
N ow this is the end of my dear tale,
D own on a lonely shore,

M e and you are friends,
E ver after happily.

Sumaiya Fatima (10)
Didcot Primary Academy, Great Western Park

My Guinea Pig Raven

Raven is quick and speedy,
But is exceptionally greedy.
He is chubby and round,
And I love it when he makes that squeaky sound.
It's so cute when he decides to play,
I love to see him every day.
He eats his lettuce leaf,
With his razor-sharp teeth.
When he hears a fox,
Raven doesn't hide in a box!
He sometimes licks,
And sometimes kicks.
He loves to have a lot of attention,
And comes running if he is mentioned.
He is my haven,
And this is my little guinea pig Raven.

Toni Arts (8)
East Sheen Primary School, London

My Family

My name is Amaar
And I can fly far.
Have you met my sister
Who can fly to Mars?
Wait, wait, wait,
Let's take a break
While I eat my chocolate cake.
It's time to get back to my awesome game
So I can show you how much I flame.
Now it's time to say goodbye
And hopefully, I will see you next time.

Amaar Rahman (11)
Eastbury Community School, Barking

This Is Me!

There once was a girl who was crazy,
She was always very lazy,
She's a girl who's sassy,
Also, she's trashy,
But her nickname was called Jassy.
This is me!

Jasmine (11)
Goddard Park Community Primary School, Swindon

This Is Me (The Unluckiest Boy On Earth)

There once was a boy called Chuk,
Who had awfully bad luck,
He fell on his face,
Got trapped in a briefcase,
Then got pecked in the face by a duck.

Chukwuemeka John (11)
Goddard Park Community Primary School, Swindon

Things I Love And Like
A kennings poem

School liker.
Singing lover.
Ballet dancer.
School talker.
Friend maker.
School walker.

Coco Yarahmadi (11)
Goddard Park Community Primary School, Swindon

Happy Day

Nearly time for breakfast and I can smell bacon and waffles
I went on a scoot with my family and had blue and pink slushies
A friendly dog went by and I got to pet it which was nice
Mummy is making pizza which is my favourite
Had my teddy close by in bed, reading Harry Potter.

Niamh Woodley (8)
Hampton Hargate Primary School, Hampton Hargate

Love

L earn to share like a mother shares the milk with the baby
O pposite to a non-sharing person like a devilish person
V ery peaceful heart that makes you as sweet as a well-scented flower
E xcept on one thing, I am a loving person.

Midun Odenusi (9)
Hampton Hargate Primary School, Hampton Hargate

This Is Who I Am

C reative as I have a big imagination
H appy like a puppy
I ntelligent as I teach my brother
Z esty and funny
A rtistic sometimes because I like to draw
R espectful to people
A mazingly flexible.

Chizara Idika (9)
Hampton Hargate Primary School, Hampton Hargate

Charlie

C harlie plays as a goalkeeper
H arry Kane shoots the ball
A lways happy
R omeo is my best friend
L ove my family
I like football
E verybody is important.

Charlie Jackson (9)
Hampton Hargate Primary School, Hampton Hargate

About Me

Who is Teniola?
She is loving and kind
She is a loving person to find
She lives with her family
Her mom's name is Folashade
Her dad's name is Tejumade
I hope our family will never fade.

Teniola Ojo (9)
Hampton Hargate Primary School, Hampton Hargate

About Me

My name is Ethan and I am nine years old
I have two sisters and one brother
And I am a Christian
The name of my school is Hampton Hargate
My teachers' names are Miss Asplin and Mrs Sullivan.

Ethan Fomoriys (9)
Hampton Hargate Primary School, Hampton Hargate

The Boy In Hampton

The boy in Hampton was worried
Because nobody was his friend
When he got home
There was a box with a husky in it
A white and black husky just for him
Now he was joyful.

Layden-Ray Beebe (9)
Hampton Hargate Primary School, Hampton Hargate

Meus Sentidos

I see with my eyes like an eagle
I listen with my ears like a bat
I smell with my nose like an elephant
I feel with my skin
I learn a lot with my senses.

Rafael Sorace Rocha (9)
Hampton Hargate Primary School, Hampton Hargate

I'm Unique

I'm unique in my own way,
I'm unique in what I say,
Now listen closely to what I tell,
Or you'll fall into a deep, dark spell.
I love mountains and going outside,
I hurt myself but I never cried.
I speak Polish and English,
But I always love a plate or a vegetable dish.

  I laugh and play all I can,
M ostly I don't have energy because I run.

U nique is always the best,
N o, my life isn't messed,
 I can't do everything at once,
Q ueues and queues just for Bounce,
U nder pressure from everything
E xcruciating pain, don't go to the king.

Poppy Przybyszewski (8)
Harris Primary Academy Mayflower, Chafford Hundred

This Is Me

I am annoying, so people say,
But I still love my family at the end of the day.
My family says I'm chatty
And that makes me snappy.
I really like basketball
But I prefer football.
I want to do zoology
But I have to study biology.
I come from the Scottish borders
So I have to follow orders.
My friend's name is Howie
And he likes David Bowie.
My other friend's name is Evan
And he is eleven.
I can't eat dairy
'Cause of my grandma, Mary.
I am called nosy,
At least I'm not studying pharmacognosy.

Benjamin Wallace (10)
Heriot Primary School, Heriot

This Is Me

My name is Archie, I like to eat
My favourite thing is to rap and beat
And I'm the kindest person you will ever meet.

I stand with Ukraine, that's not a joke
I'm really good with dogs, what a bloke!
In fact, I'm loved by all the folk.

An amazing footballer, what a goal!
Celebrate with a forward roll
Everyone says I'm a good wee soul.

My name is Archie and that is me
I bet you now want to invite me round for tea
Yippee, yippee, yippee!

Archie James Mieduniecki (9)
Heriot Primary School, Heriot

This Is Me

Book bug
Creative creator
Tired to the extreme
Helpful helper
Trustworthy truster
Organised organiser
Clumsy carrot
Chatty, chocolate chomper
Thoughtful thinking machine
Angelic angel
Shy shopper
Friendly friend
Lazy llama
Who am I?
I am me!

Katie Robertson (10)
Heriot Primary School, Heriot

Maya

M aths is better, I like it. It can be hard, it can be easy
A mazed very easily because I see a lot of amazing stuff
Y ummy Slushies. I love them. Cold days, hot days, I don't care
A t swimming, underwater is easy, above it is hard... I am learning.

Maya Bennie (8)
High Mill Primary School, Carluke

Kylah

K eep trying my best
Y esterday, I got a new puppet that looks like me
L oves to swim which is me
A lways working hard
H appy when I get something.

Kylah Hunter (8)
High Mill Primary School, Carluke

How To Create Your Own Child

What you need
One bucket of different emotions
One gallon of kindness
One bucket of creativity
One Disney film
One copy of an anime
One copy of Minecraft
An image of a YouTuber
One PC
One copy of Doom Eternal
The letter R
Three splashes of intelligence
Black fur from a Labrador
Two brown marbles
Two green marbles
A sign of the word, Libra

What to do:
Step one: Get a large bowl and pour in the bucket of emotions.

Step two: Splash the intelligence on top.
Step three: Put in the sign of the Libra zodiac.
Step four: Carefully put in the letter R
Step five: Sprinkle on the dog's hair to create a dog along with the child.
Step six: Drop on the green and brown marbles to give the child and dog eyes.
Step seven: Pour on the creativity for the child.
Step eight: Drop the games, anime and the image onto the other ingredients.
Step nine: Carefully put on the PC.
And *poof!*
You have a child and a dog!
Hope you have a wonderful day with these two!

Rian Gibson (10)
Hob Moor Primary Academy, Acomb

This Is Me

D etermined for work
Y oung
L oving as a banana
A star
N ever giving up on football

L oving as a Liverpool fan
A mazing
M agical
B rave as Mo Salah
E very car my dad has, I like
R eally big Liverpool fan
T rue friend.

Dylan Lambert (10)
Hob Moor Primary Academy, Acomb

This Is Me

To make me, you need
A dash and blob of cheese pizza
I am blonde
I am funny
I am a big fan of horses
I am tall
I love playing with my friends
I love going out with my family
I love going out with my mum, dad, my three brothers and my two sisters.

Ella Price-Bestford
Hob Moor Primary Academy, Acomb

This Is Me

I am

- **H** allie
- **A** nd I love food
- **L** ike drawing ghosts with guns
- **L** iteracy is not my favourite subject
- **I** love reading Harry Potter books
- **E** very time I'm bored, I read Harry Potter

- **W** rench is my surname
- **R** ed liquorice is delicious
- **E** nglish is my favourite subject
- **N** o. I don't like comprehension
- **C** omprehension is my least favourite
- **H** allie is my name.

Hallie Wrench (10)
Holy Child Primary School, Creggan Estate

This Is Me

H appy I am when I am doing a bar routine
A mazing is what I am at swimming
N eat at writing but that is what my mum says
N ice to all my friends - I guess I am the best one
A lot of patience waiting for my dinner
H andy as an elf doing the housework.

Hannah Morrissey
Holy Family Primary School, Downpatrick

My Life

Hello, my name is Aiden
My favourite food is plantain and fish
My friends are Francis, Lily, Jaziah, Alarnah, Kasai, Jacob, Dontae, Jesse, Raphel, Sammy, Liam and Chester
My favourite console is Xbox One
My favourite game is FIFA 22 on the Xbox One.

Aiden Moyo (9)
Holy Rosary & St Anne's Catholic Primary School, Leeds

This Is Me

To create me you will need:
A super cheesy burger
A Beanie Boo-filled bedroom
A pinch of fun and laughter
Two adorable kittens
A bunch of Squishmallows

Now you need to:
Add a pinch of fun and laughter
Mix in a bunch of Beanie Boos
Stir roughly after adding two adorable kittens
Next, add a super cheesy burger to the mix
Spread the mix over a tray neatly
Cook until glazed and fun-filled bubbles can be seen
Sprinkle on Squishmallows and leave to cool down.
This is me!

Maddie Young (9)
Ilfracombe CE Junior School, Ilfracombe

My Perfect Day

One splash of joy
One sprinkle of sand on the beach
A dash of heatwave
One lump of springtime weather
Two huge tubs of bubblegum ice cream
Three huge tubs of red Pringles
One picnic on the beach watching the sunset

This is my perfect day.

Kolby Owen (9)
Ilfracombe CE Junior School, Ilfracombe

This Is Me

A kennings poem

I am a
Fudge eater
Oreo gobbler
Oreo milkshake sipper
Hot chocolate gobbler
Dog cuddler
Music lover
Tidy bedroom fleer
Football lover
Maths master
And finally
A team sports player.

Leo Dainty (8)
Ilfracombe CE Junior School, Ilfracombe

This Is Me

My name is Paule
I'm ten and a half
I'm very precious
And the others are jealous

My favourite colour is purple
And I rescue turtles
I like to swim in the sea
With the colourful fish, I can see

When I look in the mirror
I see the me
No one else can be

This is me
And that's who I want to be.

Codaccioni Paule (11)
International School Of Gabon Ecole Ruban Vert, Gabon

Amazing Me

F rancesca is my name
R efreshing it is, I love it
A mazing me
N ice and sweet I am
C alm and sleepy I am
E arth is my mom
S ay 'yes', say 'no'
C all me if a problem rises
A problem-solver, I am!

Francesca Sernia (11)
International School Of Gabon Ecole Ruban Vert, Gabon

This Is Me!

You will need:
Five dogs and three cats,
A pinch of pink,
A swimming pool of chips,
One litre of fun,
A handful of chocolate,
Numbers to decorate.

Now you need to:
Put five dogs and three cats into a big bowl.
Add a pinch of pink and mix it in with a swimming pool of chips.
Stir in one litre of fun.
Pour into a tin and bake in the oven.
Sprinkle with glitter and decorate with chocolate numbers.
This is me!

Sienna McConnell-Elliott (9)
Irish Society's Primary School, Coleraine

This Is Me!
A kennings poem

I am a...
Football player,
Television watcher,
Lego creator,
Metal detector,
Cat lover,
Star Wars trooper,
Liverpool supporter,
Spider killer,
This is me!

Ben Linton (9)
Irish Society's Primary School, Coleraine

My Favourite Things

Let me introduce myself
My name is James
I love playing video games
But when I'm playing video games
I become hangry
And then I take a deep breath in
And a deep breath out
And I think of my favourite things
Then I become funny, caring
Wise, honest and kind-hearted
Also, when I get hangry, I eat calmly
So I wouldn't get more hangry
Otherwise, I would be very angry
When I eat I have to go to bed
I think about my favourite things
That I did that day
And after a while
I remember everything I did that day
I played football.

James Ezekiel Andrews (9)
ISML Primary (International School Michel Lucius),
Luxembourg

My Name Is Yassin

Y ellow is my favourite colour
A uman is my little brother
S alah is the best football player
S ometimes I like to spend time with my family
I slam and being Muslim is my religion
N uggets are so delicious.

Yassin Serroukh (8)
Jessop Primary School, Herne Hill

Daisy

D aisy, like the flower
A mazing, like a busy buzzing bee
I ntelligent, like a lion
S ignificant, like a view off a high cliff
Y oung, with lots more left to discover.

Daisy Daly
Kilgraston School, Bridge Of Earn

All About Me

Nathan is the kind of person who likes to play with his friends
He likes to go to family parties and doesn't like to leave when the party ends
He likes to play football but doesn't like to lose, winning is so much more fun
Video games involve others and he likes to play one on one
His brothers can be a pain and cause a lot of trouble
But when it comes to family, he will always stick up for them
No one can break the Pritchard family bubble.

Nathan Pritchard (11)
Kintore Primary School, Kintore

The Day I Stepped Onto The Ice

I remember the day I first stepped onto the ice,
I heard the crunching sound of my skates and it felt so nice.

It was then that I knew I was in love with the sport,
The ice rink was my home, not a football pitch or basketball court.

I still remember playing my first game,
After that, I hoped one day I could reach fame.

As I play on the wing
I hope I will bring plenty more wins to the team.

Every other team can only dream to be as good as us.

Evan Ness (12)
Kirkcaldy West Primary School, Kirkcaldy

Cheese

There's only one thing you need to know about me
My favourite thing in the world is cheese

I love the taste so much I would never
Throw it to waste ever

I like the way it feels if I touch it
It would heal me back up

I like the way it looks I would
Make some books about it

I will never stop eating cheese
Especially in the breeze

And that's why I like cheese
And I am going to buy some now!

Benjamin Clayton (11)
Kirkcaldy West Primary School, Kirkcaldy

Anime

Anime is my favourite animation
It has many different fascinations

My favourite anime is Dragon Ball Z
When I watch it I am filled with glee

A character I love is Naruto
When I watch it my feelings go to Pluto

I have watched anime for about a year
When a new one comes out I will hear.

Abderrahmane Braham Chaouch (11)
Kirkcaldy West Primary School, Kirkcaldy

Millie

M y friends are very fun
I love being with my family
L ots of fun with my sister
L aughing with my cousins
I nteresting talks with parents
E very day is a fun day.

Millie June Ovens (11)
Kirkcaldy West Primary School, Kirkcaldy

Me

E njoying my life
T alented and persevering
H aving a great time learning new things every day
A nd getting better at new skills
N ot letting myself down.

Ethan Learmonth (11)
Kirkcaldy West Primary School, Kirkcaldy

My Stuffies

My name is Teddy and I'm almost always ready,
I love my two lions, Lion and Lion Two and,
I have a cow named Mooshroom,
And I assure you my poem is all true.

Teddy Gadalla
Logie Primary School, Dunphail

This Is Me!

T hese are my funny friends, Duncan, Adam and Daniel
H i, my name is Stanlie.
I n football I am as fast as a cheetah.
S adie, my sister is annoying.

I n boxing and ice hockey
"S uiii!" goes Ronaldo when he scores.

M y mum and dad are the best.
E very night my dinner is delicious.

Stanlie Leslie (9)
Loreburn Primary School, Dumfries

Football

I am running rogue
Through the rows
Shooting my shot
Through your soul
I scuffed the shot
And hit the bar
And angrily smashed the rebound
And scored the goal
I did the SIUUUUU!

The ball flying through the air
Jumping high into the air
Legs towards the sky
Smashing the ball
Flying towards the net
The keeper was frozen
The net was ripped
The crowd went wild!

Next day I feel happy
Putting on my favourite shirt
Ronaldo on the back

Dreaming of playing with him
I put on FIFA and imagine away!

Jake Gray (11)
Loretto Junior School, Musselburgh

Me

I am an artist, doing great sketches
I am a boxer with a great right hook
I am a cheetah, strong and fast
I am a basketball player with a fantastic three-pointer
I am a pitbull, strong and fierce
Finally, I am a deep sleeper
And not even my mum can wake me.

Jak Donnison (11)
Manston Primary School, Crossgates

Me!

I am a happy helper
Art is my superpower
I have fast feet
I like to eat

I am a laugh maker
I am a deep sleeper
Some days are good and I'll make you smile
Some days are bad but not for long
Because I'm a superstar, and this is me.

Lily Turner (10)
Manston Primary School, Crossgates

My Poem About Me

I am as kind as Miss Thorpe
I am as clever as an ant
I am as happy as a puppy
I am as loud as a dog
I am as funny as a comedian
I am as helpful as a dictionary
I am as sporty as an athlete
No one else can be me.

Sophie May Croft (11)
Manston Primary School, Crossgates

Rap About Me

I like football
I am not very tall
I am medium size
I love French fries
I don't like peas
I don't like blue cheese
I don't like a cold breeze
I hate hurting my knees
That's all about me.

Lewis Clayton (10)
Manston Primary School, Crossgates

Princess For A Day

If I were a princess for a day
I'd wake up and shout, "Yippee! Hooray!"
I would slip on my prettiest gown
And top it off with a sparkly crown
Outside my window, I would hear a neigh!
And decide to ride my pony all day
I'd feed him lovely, sweet sugar lumps
We'd gallop around, leaping over jumps
I'd ask my friends to come for high tea
And sit underneath the apple tree
We'd eat cakes, crisps and sandwiches
We'd chat just like real princesses do
At night, there would be a royal ball
I'd wear my fanciest dress of all
I'd sing and dance and laugh and play
If only I were a princess for a day.

Aroosh Haider
Marshfield Primary School, Little Horton

I Am Hafsah-Aiman!

I like sunflowers,
They stand tall and bright,
Darkness, thunder and lightning,
Gives me a fright,
But nothing will stop me,
I'll be as high as a kite,
I am Hafsah-Aiman!
I don't hide behind my glasses,
I am confident in my classes,
And hopefully this will get me passes,
I am Hafsah-Aiman!
I like noodles,
And sometimes poodles,
And now it's time for me to say toodles...
I am Hafsah-Aiman!
I look in the mirror,
And what do I see...?
I see the person,
No one else can be,
I am Hafsah-Aiman!

All I see...
Is the future footballer I aim to be,
Ronaldo is the person who inspires me,
I am Hafsah-Aiman!
I like learning Arabic,
I started during the pandemic,
I struggle as it is challenging,
But the language is so aesthetic,
I am Hafsah-Aiman!

Hafsah-Aiman Younas (8)
Marshfield Primary School, Little Horton

Snowflake, Snowflake

Snowflake, snowflake from up in the sky
You're so blue and up in the sky
Why are you so beautiful and so amazing
Snowflake, snowflake, let's make a snowman today?
Snowflake, snowflake, let's play
Let's play in the snow and rain
Snowflake, snowflake, how are you today?
Snowflake, snowflake, up in the sky at midnight
Let's go and catch snowflakes
Snowflake, snowflake, come on and let's play again
Why do you go up so high in the blue sky?
You're so beautiful
Snowflake, snowflake, you're so beautiful like a beautiful clear sky up so high.

Amima Butt (8)
Marshfield Primary School, Little Horton

The Food Poem

Self-raising flour - I like to help people rise
Chocolate - I am sweet and like to make people happy
Milk - I like to give people strength when they are upset
Tea - I like to help people relax and have a break
Food - I like to bring people together
This is me!

Hajirah Hussain (8)
Marshfield Primary School, Little Horton

Special Person

My name is Azaan,
I am 9 years old,
I like the colour blue,
And I am good at maths.

Azaan Ahmed (9)
Marshfield Primary School, Little Horton

Friends And Family

F riends make me laugh and run
R eally fast and make me happy when
I am sad, when I am sad they come up to me
E very day I go to school, my friends always by me
N ight-time I always go to bed, joyfully happy, I had
D essert in the school hall. I saw my friends. The
S chool teacher said, "It's the end of play." My

F amily took me home. I saw my rabbit and did some
A rt in my room, then my mum said, "It is time for tea."
M y mum and dad were going out, so my brother looked after me
I n my room I did some colouring and painting
L ooking at my art book I coloured a rabbit in
"Y ummy dessert," I said to my mum. "It is homemade."

Grace Beer (8)
Model Church In Wales Primary School, Carmarthen

I'm A Lucky Girl

I'm a clever girl
And I'm a lucky girl.
I'm a super, super fast girl.
My maths is so cool.
I like this world very much.
When I grow up
I will go to NASA.
I will go to the sun
And I will go to Pluto.
I'm going to be very popular
In this beautiful world.

Dihansa Dewsiluni Manamperi (8)
Model Church In Wales Primary School, Carmarthen

My Haiku Poetry, Cats Rule

I have three cool cats
One's called Foz and one's called Fern
And Mini Marble!

I love tiger cubs
Cats, brilliant and so fun
I love snow leopards.

I live in a house
A house with my family
And with my cool... cats!

Isabel Otterburn (9)
Model Church In Wales Primary School, Carmarthen

The Gaming Poem

L ooking at games is my thing
U ndoing my mistakes in Minecraft, yea
C asing who destroyed my secret base
A nd my wolf is so cute you
S ay, "Hey," in chat, "this is me!"

E teled is my favourite Wii skin
L ying on my bed going, "Sweet"
I never lose in Obby's, even difficult charts

H ey, this is me! This is sweet
A nd again and again I 'find the markers', always get markers every day
R arities/fairies are my things, Lankybox please thank me
G etting Netherite from another
R aving to Crab Rave and Lankybox Milk Song
A yo friends at school being sussy
V olume on Xbox 100%
E ach time I play my destiny awaits.

Lucas-Eli Hargrave (9)
Motcombe CE VA Primary School, Shaftesbury

This Is Me

T he best teacher is my teacher
H ave some habits and some allergies
O utside I don't play tennis
M y hobby is football
A s much as I love my dad I love my mum
S o here I come to enter the competition

R ight now I want to be a builder
I like school
C ould I win? I don't know
H ere I come for the bookmark
E arning prizes is my favourite thing
N ow you may not have heard of me, but I'm pretty cool
S nakes are my favourite animal.

Thomas Richens (9)
Motcombe CE VA Primary School, Shaftesbury

I'm Like A Magic Potion!

These are the things that make me, me,
Because of these properties, I give people such glee!
These things make me glow,
I hope my poem can flow.

I think I'm poetic,
I think I'm very energetic,
I think I'm very lucky,
I think I'm very funny.

I like Terry,
She's as sour as a berry,
I like Jerry,
She's got cute miaows!

Summer Robertson (9)
Motcombe CE VA Primary School, Shaftesbury

Me

Being friendly is my thing,
Though I don't like wearing bling.

My friends say I am really smart,
They also say I have a big heart.

Sometimes I will rewind,
When my friends aren't being kind.

I am really tall,
I like watching football.

I have great friends and family,
They all mean so much to me.

I really love watching sheep,
Especially when they are asleep.

Betsy Billings (9)
North Hinksey CE Primary School, North Hinksey

All About Me

I love pets
But I don't really like pests.
I love nature
But I don't think I hate ya!
I love reading
But I don't really like bleeding.
I like feeding
But I don't really like weeding.

Amelia Wing (9)
North Hinksey CE Primary School, North Hinksey

It's Normal To Cry

My favourite thing about myself is that I help people when they need help.
Ingredients that you will need to make me is a bit of sugar for my craziness
But make sure not to spill any otherwise I become annoying.
You will need some salt for my moodiness that comes once in a while.
My dream future is to become an archaeologist or be a famous book writer
To show people that you can cry without being a crybaby, it's normal to cry.
What I love to do when I'm sad is to stare into space
And dream or speak to my best friend, Daisy Hackett.
My colour would be yellow for my happiness.
Dancing, playing and moving is the only definition of me.

Emily McGimpsey (11)
Northcote Primary School, Liverpool

Me And The Things I Love

T oday when I get home I will play on a game called Ark.
H appily, I learn about animals to protect them.
I hope that one day I will get a snake as a pet.
S omeday I will become an animal rescuer.

I have an incredible imagination.
S o many creative ideas are in my brain.

M y favourite thing to do is to look at scary, slimy snake pictures.
E agerly, I am writing my amazing acrostic poem.

Reuben Wright (7)
Oasis Academy Marksbury Road, Bristol

I Love School

T omorrow it's a really fun day - PE day!
H appily, I go to school because I love it.
I am so happy today because I am going to a pool tomorrow!
S omeday I wish I could be a football player.

I t's just so close to PE time and I am super excited!
S uper, super excited!

M y favourite thing is playing fun, fantastic football!
E agerly, I also play superhero games.

Oscar Watkins (6)
Oasis Academy Marksbury Road, Bristol

Jelani The Sportsman

T oday, I am going to wear my purple and black, shiny football boots
H ere is where I play football at Hengrove and I support a team called Manchester United
I love kicking footballs
S omeday, I would like to be a sportsman

I love playing with my friend, Hugo
S omeday, I would like to be a sportsman

M y brother helps me on Fortnite
E cstatically, I play basketball.

Jelani Ricketts (6)
Oasis Academy Marksbury Road, Bristol

Me And My Cat

T omorrow I am going to golf.
H appily, I helped Mum when we were making a great breakfast.
I went on holiday on Monday. It was amazing and beautiful
S ome days I rapidly run back home and rush to get on my Nintendo.

I am fun and amazing and smart.
S omeday I want to be a policeman.

M e and my dad play fabulous football.
E agerly, I run to the Muga at playtime.

Lorenzo Sutera (7)
Oasis Academy Marksbury Road, Bristol

Me And My Dog

T oday, I am at my lovely classroom with my lovely friends.
H appily, I see my lovely, cute, soft dog.
I love playing with my friends, Oliver and Oscar.
S ometimes, I like playing on my Nintendo Switch.

I n my home, I like playing with my Venom action figure.
S ome days, I watch TV.

M y dog is very playful and soft.
E agerly, I am writing amazing poems.

Klay Walton (7)
Oasis Academy Marksbury Road, Bristol

All About Abdil

T oday, I'm dreaming about going swimming
H appily, I go underwater to scare people
I 'm going to Paris next time
S ome day, I'm going to the beach

I n the summer holidays, I am going to CBeebies Land!
S omeday, CBeebies Land is closed

M ost days, I go to Asda to buy something
E xcitedly, I go to Taco Bell and it makes me ecstatic.

Abdilatif Abiib (7)
Oasis Academy Marksbury Road, Bristol

The Wings I Love

T oday I am going to my incredible school!
H appily, tomorrow I am going to a giant shop.
I am going swimming at the weekend.
S ometimes I relax in my big, giant house.

I am amazing and funny.
S ometimes I go to the park.

M y favourite thing to do is to play football at the park,
E very time I am bored I go to my nanny's house.

Tommy Singleton (6)
Oasis Academy Marksbury Road, Bristol

This Is Me

T omorrow, I am going to play out with my dad
H appily, I want to play tennis with my mum and dad
I 'm good as a goalie
S omeday, I want to play football

I n summer, I want to have ice cream
S omeday, I want to be a football and basketball player.

M y favourite thing is my big, beautiful cat
E very day, I am kind to my friends.

Gabriel Magro (7)
Oasis Academy Marksbury Road, Bristol

Exciting Things That I Love

T oday, I am going out and playing games
H opefully, Ariana is coming to my house
I love bunnies because I had one
S ecretly, I look out for my friends so I know that they are okay

I am seven on May the 13th
S ometimes I love playing Minecraft

M y cousin Charle is in the same school as me
E ncanto is my favourite movie.

Lily Fletcher-Wilmut (6)
Oasis Academy Marksbury Road, Bristol

Me And The Things I Love

T oday, I am going to a great school
H appily, I am helping my daddy
I am going to after school club
S ometimes, I get annoyed

I 'm fantastic, hard-working and epic
S omeday, I am going to be a farmer or a shepherd

M y favourite thing to do is play on the computer
E agerly, I write my incredible poem.

Jacoby Cunningham (7)
Oasis Academy Marksbury Road, Bristol

Adventure With My Dogs

T oday, I'm going boxing with my strong friend
H appily, I walk to my friend's house
I like to sit with my friends at lunchtime
S ometimes, I go to basketball with my dad

I n the future, I have PE
S omeday, I want to be a boxer

M y favourite thing is doing PE
E agerly, I write my outstanding work.

Leyland Chard (7)
Oasis Academy Marksbury Road, Bristol

Me, My Sister And The Things I Love

T oday, I am going swimming because my mum booked it
H appily, I walk down the path
I 've been good so I have some money
S ometimes, I see my beautiful family

I am funny, smart and epic
S omeday I want to be a shopkeeper

M y sister's name is Isabella
E very day I go to a kind, colourful school!

Imogen Tinline (7)
Oasis Academy Marksbury Road, Bristol

Me And The Things I Love

T he cat in my garden is furry and cute
H appily, I slide down a slide
I 'd really like to be a hairdresser
S miling and laughing, I swim around

I am excellent, lovely and friendly
S ome day, I'd like a sleepover

M y favourite thing to do is play
E agerly, I write my unique and wonderful poem.

Esme Forsyth (6)
Oasis Academy Marksbury Road, Bristol

Taihir's Life

T oday, I want to go to after school club
H appily, I like to play on my Nintendo
I adore being a game creator
S omeday, I would like to see my cousin, Rai

I n the summer, I would like to get some sun
S uperbly, I am fantastic

M y friends would say I tell the best jokes
E very day, I play on my iPad.

Taihir Medley-Hutchins (7)
Oasis Academy Marksbury Road, Bristol

All About Joey

T oday, I'm playing with a beautiful black and white cat
H appily, I play football with my friends
I 'm brave, funny and sporty
S ometimes, I play basketball

I play handball
S oon, I'm going to the park

M ost days, I play dodgeball
E agerly, I rush home to play on my Nintendo Switch.

Joey Parsons (6)
Oasis Academy Marksbury Road, Bristol

Me And The Things I Love

T oday, I'm going to rush home to play with my brother
H appily, I help my brother play Fortnite
I 'm good at Fortnite
S ometimes I go to shows

I am incredible, funny and amazing
S oon is Victorian day

M y incredible, playful brother plays with me
E very day, I play on my PS4.

Oliver Morgan (7)
Oasis Academy Marksbury Road, Bristol

My Favourite Things

T oday, I am going to see beautiful brown horses
H opefully, I will go to Lily's house
I love bouncing on bouncy castles
S ome day, I will have two babies

I 'm eight on December the 13th
S ometimes, I love Pac-Man

M y gymnastics is brilliant
E ncanto is my favourite movie.

Ariana Timinskaite (7)
Oasis Academy Marksbury Road, Bristol

Life Of A Lady

T oday, I am writing happily
H ow did people get brought to Earth? I wonder
I like to read Bunny vs Monkey
S ometimes I play the piano

I like it when it's quiet
S ome people think differently

M y absolute favourite thing is science
E sme is my best friend.

Sylvie Frazier-Brown (7)
Oasis Academy Marksbury Road, Bristol

This Is Me

T oday, I am going to the park
H appily, I go to school
I am brave
S ometimes I like to play at school

I like maths because it's easy
S ometimes I like to play

M ost times I like playing
E agerly, I come to school.

Sophia Smith (7)
Oasis Academy Marksbury Road, Bristol

The Window

T here, a window stood dirty and boarded up.
H e stared, between the cracks. A dark, tall figure.
E ven when the night sky,

W ould flood the gardens,
I see white eyes peered through.
N ever leaving, as I cry.
D oesn't it feel odd?
O h of course it did.
W hy, why wouldn't my reflection copy?

Isabella Angell (12)
Park Community School, Leigh Park

Light Somebody's Day

A haiku

Football is equal,
Let's be in - to kick it out,
Light somebody's day.

Joshua Musasa
Park Community School, Leigh Park

This Is Who I Am

T all in size.
H appy every day.
I love playing games.
S o loving.

I love my dad, he is my hero.
S o cuddly and really funny.

M e and my dad play.
E gyptians are my favourite topic.

This is me.

Shivam Solanki (8)
Park School For Girls, Ilford

Me And My Food

My favourite food is a Pot Noodle
It makes me want to doodle
My favourite flavour is beef
Sometimes it gets stuck in my teeth
I like to have something sweet
It makes me dance and tap my feet
I like to have a drink
It is Vimto and it is pink.

Thomas Mac Lockley (8)
Parkwood Primary School, Keighley

This Is Me

K arting is the best motorsport
A ll motorsports are fun but karting is more fun
R iding makes me feel joy
T yres make the kart move
I t makes me shine when I ride
N ever give up on karting
G o-karting is the best, I always help my dad fix my kart.

Berri-Rae Pryor (8)
Ponsbourne St Mary's CE Primary School, Hertford

Beach Time

B oats on the sea
E veryone is playing in the sea
A seagull steals chicken and chips
C rabs run over tall, small, wavy waves
H ot day on the beach.

Ava Sims (8)
Ponsbourne St Mary's CE Primary School, Hertford

The Rainbow Unicorn And The Small Girl

The girl skipped along the green grass with her colourful unicorn
The girl's eyes were blue like the blue wavy ocean
She wore a red and orange dress that look like a hot fire burning
She had a yellow hat that shone brightly as the sun
She was ten years old and her name was Emily
When I saw the girl I was so shocked that she had a unicorn
So went to her and we played a lovely game with the unicorn
She liked pizza and for a drink she drank Coke
She also ate very quickly and then she sadly said goodbye.

Waslat Saberi (8)
Radford Academy, Radford

Kindness Is As Bright As The Light Which Makes Our Day

M y life is like this
O h my life can be wonderful or bad
M y life cannot be perfect
I can muddle my emotions all around me
N o one's life is like another
A nd yet again everyone's different from others
H ow rude people are to point, stare or say mean things
S o it's not people's fault how they look, walk or talk

P eople can't make themselves perfect
O h people wish they can change themselves to become normal
E veryone is different, there's no such thing as normal
M y, wouldn't life be boring if we were all the same?

Mominah Mohammed (9)
Rosedale Primary School, Hayes

This Is Me!

My family and friends make me cheerful
And my cousins are quite playful,
But my favourite thing about me is
My arts and crafts and not being smart.

Can you guess who I want to be when I grow up?
A famous archaeologist and to travel the world!

Try and answer this riddle,
Who do you think I admire?
He lives with me,
He is a grown-up
And looks after me and my brother.
He has a family.
Who is he?

Saina Langani (10)
Rosedale Primary School, Hayes

This Is Me

Happiness is a great emotion.
What is in this potion?
Writing the racism poem was fun,
I was even thrilled when I found out I won!

Anger is a lion ready to pounce,
That's my emotion when silly people play about.
When I'm agitated I get very aggrieved.
Bitter, bitter is like litter.

Calm is a huge soft pillow,
It reminds me of willows,
Soft and delicate.

Sachleen Kaur (10)
Rosedale Primary School, Hayes

This Is Me!

This is me,
I am annoying like a droid
Trying to find my way out of anger like a drone.
Should I be angry?
Should I be kind?
My emotions will decide.
Anger is from the deepest depths of Hell
While my friend, Kindness, is from the highest skies of Heaven.
Which should I be?
My emotions will decide!

Ahmed Ali Shahid (10)
Rosedale Primary School, Hayes

This Is Me

My favourite character is Peppa
My favourite person is my aunt
My favourite entertainment is games
My favourite place is London
My personality is loving
My favourite colour is yellow
My favourite food is McDonald's
If I was an animal, I would be a frog.

Harmilton O Agbota Okungbor (14)
Rosehill School, Nottingham

Doctor

D octors serve us day and night
O h, to this world, they bring the light
C ares for people when we are in need
T o make us healthy and strong indeed
O ne who makes most diseases cure
R eally, I want to pursue this for sure!

Dhanvanthkrishnan Saravanan (7)
Saint Xavier Nursery And Primary School, India

This Is Me!

Funny and kind, this is me
Sporty and active, this is me
Sunny and cold, this is me
Spring is my favourite season, this is me
Friendly and competitive, this is me
My favourite colours are blue, yellow and green
Love the colour of the night sky
My favourite animal is a dog, this is me
Tall with braids, this is me
Like me and this is me
I like ice cream and doughnuts, this is me.

Renee Appiah-Kubi (10)
Salisbury Manor Primary School, Chingford

How To Make Me!

Firstly, add two teaspoons of sass.
Next, add four jugs full of creativity.
Then add two jugs full of 'I'm totally paying attention'.
Then splash in three cups of 'I'm so sporty'.
Once you've done that, mix them in a bowl.
After that, add half a cup of dumbness,
Then infinite amounts of kindness,
One cup full of fast thinking,
A whole 20 cups full of talent,
Four cups full of singing talent,
Eight jugs full of emo style,
Nine cups of 'I am totally the best gamer',
Four cups full of comedian,
Five cups full of rebel,
And lastly, 11 cups of bookworm-ness.
When you put them in the bowl,
Mix them in a blender,
Then you get me!

Layla West (9)
Sandown Primary School, Deal

I Am Eden

I am Eden,
I like ice cream cold,
I'm not from Sweden,
I like to work as a team.

Amazing, kind friend,
An animal lover,
Arts and crafts person,
Also, I like times tables.

My BFF is Delilah,
Magnificent maths whizz,
Marshmallows are sweet and delicious,
Making cakes is my favourite hobby.

   E lephants are my second-favourite animal,
   D aisies are my favourite flowers,
   E xpress all my feelings to Delilah,
   N ature friendly, yes I am.

Eden Cope-Lamb (9)
Sandown Primary School, Deal

How To Make Me!

To create me, you will need:
1 bird feather,
1tsp of fluff,
2 sausages,
1 scary video game,
1 potato.

Now you need to:
Now put the fluff and bird feather into a bowl and mix together.
Then put the sausages, potato and scary video game into another bowl.
Now put the two mixes together and stir for ten minutes.
Then put it in the oven for ten minutes.
Take it out and... You have me!

Rae Young (9)
Sandown Primary School, Deal

This Is Me!

I am brave, yet I'm still young,
But I'm fierce like a lion cub,
I love to play rugby,
Some people may think it's muck,
But if I have no luck,
Just come on,
People are calling me a duck,
Sometimes I am a mischievous person in school,
Although I think mermaids are pretty cool,
And I can make cute cards that are handmade,
And finally, this is me!

Daisy Todd (9)
Sandown Primary School, Deal

Who Am I?

I am as funny as a clown,
I have a sky-blue dressing gown.
My hair is as orange as fire,
Honest and never a liar.
I like to play Fortnite,
Also, I like to give people a fright.
I am very kind,
In school, I have a big mind.
And when I am always in my house,
I always see a mouse.
Who am I?

Answer: Charlie James Reid.

Charlie James Reid (9)
Sandown Primary School, Deal

Learning Riddle

Some kids love it, some hate it,
I go there most days,
Sometimes it's as confusing as a maze.

Sometimes stressful, others calm,
Sometimes I'm bored or having fun,
It's probably number one.

What is it?

Answer: School.

Finley Lawson (9)
Sandown Primary School, Deal

This Is Me

I'm a boy
With a mouth and eyes
And just now I realise

I'm good at football
Running and more
But I always forget
To shut my bedroom door

I love Fortnite
I love food
Even when I'm in a bad mood

I'm a boy
With a mouth and eyes
And just now I realise.

Henry Rudd (10)
South Wootton Junior School, South Wootton

Facts

F antastic
A rthur
C alton
T all
S o this is me

B rother and sister
O scar is my brother
Y ou should be my friend.

Arthur Calton (9)
South Wootton Junior School, South Wootton

This Is Me

C ats
A pple
L aughing is funny
E ggs are not yummy
B ut chocolate ones are good

W ater is yummy.

Caleb W (11)
South Wootton Junior School, South Wootton

This Is Me

I am kind
I am a nice person
I am good at Minecraft
I am polite
I am funny
I am fun to be around.

Eli Ssekabuzza (9)
South Wootton Junior School, South Wootton

She Says

She says
What's something you like about yourself?
Ask my friends or my enemies

She says
What's your least favourite thing in the world?
Go to someone I hate

She says
What's your favourite thing?
It's as yellow as the sun, salty like the sea

She says
What's your most used emotion?
Yeah, don't ask.

Eva Ansley (8)
Springfield Primary School, Rowley Regis

Here Is Me

I am kind and creative
I have a smart mind
Although I fall down
I try not to frown
Though I get hurt
My mom makes me better with dessert
I love my family
My family have a caring personality
I love sports
I always help my teammates with support
Though I may not be good at things in life
I try my best to shine bright.

Eliza Bates (9)
Springfield Primary School, Rowley Regis

What Do I Like The Most?

I love to listen to calming music,
It makes me as sleepy as a deer.
I like to pet animals every time I see one.
I love watching the sunset,
As it goes as dark as the deep blue sea.
My family are the most beautiful family in the world.
I love playing with my best friends,
Because they're as beautiful as a sunflower.

Vanessa Disley (7)
St Benedict's Catholic Primary School, Hindley

A Recipe To Make You Spectacular

First, pour in positivity, then
Add a dash of kindness.
Fold in a spoonful of goodwill.
Dissolve a heart full of love.
Next, mix awesomeness
A bunch of truthfulness.
Include a cup of jolly fun.
Stir in a personal goal.
Then chop in equal parts negativity.
For extra flavour, add an extra-large smile.
A teaspoon of goodwill.
Bake mixture at 500 degrees for eight years.
Allow forgiveness to sink in and happiness.
Sprinkle blissfulness and
This is me!

Yousaf Ali (8)
St Bride's Primary School, Bothwell

A Recipe To Make You Happy

First, pour in a cup of kindness.
Next add a spoonful of calmness.
Fold in a spoonful of truth.
Dissolve some forgiveness.
Next, mix in awesomeness.
Then add a bunch of courage.
Next sprinkle a bit of love.
Include a cup of forgiveness.
Stir some motivation.
For extra flavour add silliness.
Then chop in equal parts
Add cuteness
Bake mixture at 500 degrees for kindness
Cook for three hours.

Chloe Meikle (8)
St Bride's Primary School, Bothwell

A Recipe To Make Me

First, pour in one kilogram of resilience.
Add a dash of awesomeness.
Dissolve one gram of shyness into confidence.
Fold in a drop of forgiveness.
Next, mix in one gram of truthfulness.
Add a bunch of funky friendship.
Then chop in equal parts of bravery.
Dissolve the bravery with the strength
Pour in one teaspoon of uniqueness.

Stella McCluskey (8)
St Bride's Primary School, Bothwell

All About Me

Tariq is my name,
Me and my friends like playing games.
Sometimes, me and family play board games.

I always do my best,
So I never fail a test.
Some people maybe not have guessed,
But I always leave my room in a mess!

I'm not a travelling person,
I've never been on a plane,
So, I haven't been to Spain.

I'm always here for my friends,
And I don't pretend.

I hope you had a nice day,
And thank you for reading my poem!

Tariq Lwanyaga (11)
St Bridget's Primary RC School, Baillieston

This Is Me Rap

The main thing about me is gymnastics
Flipping around the place now, it's fantastic
When I do a skill I turn elastic
Like I just said, I am fantastic

I also love animals, they are the best
I love sheep, there is no contest
I have a little lamb called Dolly
She is so cute, she gets pushed in a trolley

Music is nice, I love Eminem
Even my lamb, she loves to sing them.

Molly-Kate O'Connor (11)
St Columb's Primary School Cullion, Desertmartin

This Is Me

This is me, I've got special eyes because God made them.
They're brown and green and I'm not ashamed of them.
I have got peach-coloured skin.
I've got freckles and am not afraid to show them.
I am in God's image, so I am always perfect.
I love myself so I love God.
I don't care if I am short because God made me and everyone else so I am happy.
So never change yourself.
Remember that God never fails, and love everyone and so love yourself!

Richard Bykowski (9)
St Helen's RC Primary School, Brixton

This Is Me

This is me,
I have black eyes,
I have brown skin,
I have fluffy hair,
I have clean teeth.

I am special at football,
I am special at basketball,
I am special at games,
I am special at maths.

Forgiving people joyfully because
This is me.

Jaydan B (9)
St Helen's RC Primary School, Brixton

Me In A Tree

I am as a tall as a giraffe
And I like to catch a ball
I love my art and also my family say I'm smart
I also like Minecraft
It's a fantastic game
And I would like to ride on my bike every day
I have a dog
He always jumps like a frog
Then I have mum and dad
And I'm ever so glad
They're mum and dad
Then I have two sisters
Sometimes they're a bit like blisters
But I love them a lot
This is me!

Amelie R (10)
St Ignatius Catholic Primary School, Ossett

This Is Me

T all as a tower
H air as brown as chocolate
I ncredibly clumsy and always falling over
S illy as fun - I love to tell jokes.

I am not very neat
S trawberry Haribos are what I love to eat.

M y only policy is that I don't cheat!
E ggs are what I don't like to eat.

This is me!

Niamh N (10)
St Ignatius Catholic Primary School, Ossett

This Is Me

K ind to everyone
I am nice and funny
N uggets are my favourite food
D igging in the garden.

C ool as a cucumber
O scar is my creative cousin
O ften we play farm animals
L ove Mum 100%.

Mason Cusworth (9)
St Ignatius Catholic Primary School, Ossett

Environment

E veryone has to keep the world clean
N obody should litter, the planet thinks it is mean
V erse by verse, everybody has to do their part
I f everybody cleans the world they must have a big heart
R oads have plastic on them which is very bad
O ceans have plastic in them as well which is very sad
N umerous plastic pieces are around the world but people don't even think
M illions of people throw litter and don't think once
E ven if we don't have a bin near us we should not litter
N ever litter, and if you see someone else, tell them not to litter
T eam up to clean the world, the world should not be bitter!

Kavya Panchal (9)
St Margaret's CE Junior School, Rainham

This Is Me!

A handful of happiness,
A bowl of joyfulness,
A cup of sadness,
A pinch of kindness,
A spoonful of loveliness,
Turn of dancing,
Add some colouring,
A bundle of friendship,
A sprinkle of reading books,
Throw in some acting,
A blend of tickling,
A stir of golf,
Pour in some horse riding,
A bundle of eco,
Crack in the beauty make-up,
And this makes me!

Ceallaigh McCrory (8)
St Mary's Primary School, Maghery

Dylan's Life

My name is Dylan,
My favourite sport is Gaelic football,
I am a boy that is 11 years old,
And I like to play a lot of games,
My best friend is Jake,
He likes most of the stuff that I like.

Dylan Convie (11)
St Mary's Primary School, Maghery

This Is Me

T urtles are my favourite animal
H orses are cute
I like to draw and I like Halloween
S eptember and October are my favourite months

I like to play with my friends
S ometimes I hate my sisters and I love horror movies

M y friends and family are the best people on Earth
E mus are my favourite bird.

Nadia Alichniewicz (10)
St Mary's RC Primary School, Swinton

This Is Phoebe

T his is me
H appy, healthy and love to cheer
I 'm very talkative as people will say
S carlett is my best friend and someone I can trust

I like to do gymnastics, flexible is a name
S ome people will say

M y name is Phoebe
E very day I'm ready to face the world.

Phoebe Gore (10)
St Mary's RC Primary School, Swinton

This Is About Me

T all in size
H elpful like my mum
I love learning more things about dinosaurs
S ometimes I can be really annoying

I can really be like an animal
S nakes are one of my favourite reptiles

M y dog is really clever and she is scared of my dad
E ating is my thing.

Jake Braphy (10)
St Mary's RC Primary School, Swinton

Things About Me

M y name is Freya
Y ou are pretty

O wn person
W ith lots of love
N ow I am born

P erson who is kind
E ating I like to do
R ight I am
S inging is my thing
O n Monday I'm lazy
N o, I don't like spiders but I like me.

Freya Darby (10)
St Mary's RC Primary School, Swinton

All About Me!

Chatting with friends is cool
Reading is fine, you need to read anyways
Eating brownies is yummy
Art is my favourite thing to do
I'm very creative with my drawings
But I hate when people look at them
Tea is nice and warm
Every day I'm mostly chaotic.

Emilia Kozlowska (9)
St Patrick's Catholic Primary School, Birmingham

This Is Me

Hi, I'm chilled on the sofa watching TV.
This is me!

My friends call me crazy!
This is me!

I love, love, love HP (Harry Potter).
This is me!

I have two besties, one is Soph and one is Gracey.
This is me!

I love and wish I had a doggy!
This is me!

I have an annoying brother called Charlie!
This is me!

I love to go swimming in the sea!
This is me!

Dad's English, Mum's Irish, don't know which I wanna be.
This is me!

I like to sing and dance crazily.
This is me!

I'm kinda sorta artsy.
This is me! This is me! This is me!

Madeline Bye (10)
St Patrick's Primary School, Hilltown

About Me

There are lots of things
That I like
And there is a lot about me
Family, friends and other things
That complete my personality.

I love doing art,
My dream is to meet Olly Murs
I support the best team, Arsenal
But definitely not Spurs.

My favourite time is Christmas
I love going on holiday
In my free time I watch Harry Potter
No more homework today
Hip hip hooray!

I play piano and tin whistle
Playing in the sun
Singing and dancing
It's all so much fun!

Emily Read (10)
St Patrick's Primary School, Hilltown

Me

My heart is full of joy and kindness,
My hair is like noodles, nice and curly head,
My brain is like a boat, it travels around my head,
My eyes are like green grass, blue sky, brown dirt,
My arms are made out of stones,
My legs are made out of wood.

Ellie Mae McGinn (10)
St Patrick's Primary School, Hilltown

Seamus

S eamus plays GAA football
E very Sunday I go to a football match
A fter school I go home to my house
M y favourite food is hot dogs and chips
U neasy about riding my bike
S eamus has blue eyes.

Seamus Barber (10)
St Patrick's Primary School, Hilltown

What's My Emotion?

I like to smile,
I like to make people laugh,
When Anger appears
You might end up in tears,
So I always try to help
Those people who need it,
So I can cheer them up.

Answer: Happiness.

Niamh Farrell (10)
St Patrick's Primary School, Hilltown

This Is Me

D arragh is my name
A nd I like sport
R eading books I like
R unning is my favourite sport
A nd I like farming
G ood at maths
H abit of jumping.

Darragh Harrison (10)
St Patrick's Primary School, Hilltown

Relaxed

Relaxed is tucked up in bed reading a nice book, fluffy and warm in bed.
Relaxed is zooming in the kitchen to do some drawing of some animals like a bunny.
Relaxed is in your warm and cosy bedroom, playing with your favourite teddies.
Relaxed is buried in fluffy blankets, watching a movie.

Olivia Ball (8)
St Peter's CE First School, Marchington

Comics

Comics are the coolest thing
They have a certain ring
My dad has a collection
It's his most prized possession
He has a special book
But he never lets me look
He has Spider-Man, Batman, Superman too!
He has dreadful ones, which will make you say boo!
The only one he's let me see
Well, that must be Spider-Man, by Ditko and Lee.
DC do the best ones,
They make me laugh and grin,
They put a smile on my ears, which started from my chin.
Comics are the best thing, I don't care what you say!
They make me smile and that's what makes my day.

Cairo Irons (11)
St Winefride's Primary School, Manor Park

This Is Me!

At the beginning of time, I was the sky
My colour changed with my emotions
But when the first life form approached the land
The home I once knew changed forever

250 million years ago, I was an ammonite swimming free
Today I am fossilised 250 miles from the sea

In the Stone Age era, I was a cavewoman
I was wistful, my hair was as silver as the stifling smoke

100 years ago, I was the tiniest acorn in my textured golden cap
Now I'm a wise, strong oak tree with seeds of millions of what I once was

On a brisk spring morning, I was a delicate pink rose
The first gift of this beautiful season

On New Year's Day, I'm an energetic Jack Russell puppy
Playing with the new beginnings

On midsummer's day, I'm a fly on the wall
Watching the school children daydreaming at an open window

In autumn, I'm a conker with my spiky armour
Just revealing my brown inner self

At night, I'm a nocturnal explorer
Discovering new species in the midnight blue

Tonight, I am a dream, tomorrow a daydream
The next day I will be a reality

Next month, I'm Jambo Wanzagi
A traveller through time

In my afterlife, I'm a scarecrow standing motionless
Watching the crows rift off into the vermillion haze

At the end of time, I was a comet racing through space
With the remains of the world spinning chaotically around me

This is me, pencil in my hand
I'm anything I want to be, anywhere, anytime

My imagination lifts me
I'm a young raven soaring into the cobalt sky.

Bonny Clutterbuck (11)
Stanton Drew Primary School, Stanton Drew

This Is Me

T he group of friends dance around
H owever I like to bounce up and down
I love to be excited every single day
S ame when it becomes Christmas time

I love to party with my kind family
S ame when I watch films and be happy

M y eyes are like blue ocean waves
E verybody keeps me smiley, so do the people that make me laugh.

Maya Milner (11)
Summerfield Primary School, Leeds

How To Make Me

To make me you will need:
A unicorn-filled bedroom.
A plate of chicken nuggets.
A sprinkle of smiling.
A pinch of fun.
A bit of happiness.
And a dash of brightness.
Here I am.

Jennifer Beaumont (8)
Summerfield Primary School, Leeds

This Is Me

When I bowl, I am fast and furious, focused and free.
This is me.

When I bat, I am strong and sturdy, super and speedy.
This is me.

When I field, I am alert and ace, awesome and amazing.
This is me.

When I am the wicket-keeper, I am focused and strong, ace and super and free.
This is me.

Manahil Zaidi (9)
Sutton High Prep School, Sutton

This Is Me!

These are my favourite things
I like pizza
I like my friends
But most importantly, I like my family
I am nearly 9
I have a pet rabbit and a dog
My rabbit is three months old
My dog is getting older.

Summer Ballard (9)
Sutton-on-Trent Primary & Nursery School, Sutton-On-Trent

What I Am!

I is for intelligent
S is for smart
A is for adventurous
B old and fearless
E is for enthusiastic
L is for loving
L is for learntastic
A is for awesome.

Isabella Brookfield (8)
The Ferncumbe CE Primary School, Hatton

Who I Am

I like ice cream, it makes me want to scream,
Every lick feels like I am in a dream.
I am a good friend, that is not pretend.
I'm always polite, I'm the opposite of a fright.
I might be funny but sometimes I'm serious,
I am not often furious.
But if you try to make me sad, I will get quite mad.
I like fluffy kittens, they are very cute,
Not much like a newt.
I would cuddle them all day,
And when I see one, I shout, "Yay, yay, yay!"

George Johnson (10)
Towers Junior School, Hornchurch

This Is Me

K ind and helpful,
A dventurer,
Y ou may think I hate maths, I don't,
D on't you think I'm slow,
E xplorer,
N ice to others.

Kayden Houghton (9)
Upton Priory School, Macclesfield

This Is Me

I am Aisha
I like standing on things
I love cats
They are special
I am as fast as a blast
I am kind and nice
I have brown hair
Be aware
You are you
I am me
I am fun and friendly
I cheer up my friends.

Aisha Drammeh (9)
Victoria Park Primary Academy, Smethwick

What Emotion Am I?

My hands are sweaty and wet
It feels like rain dropping on my head
I think I feel like I haven't been fed
Winter is when the light fades fast and Christmas is on its way
With kids full of excitement, waiting for that magical day
Autumn is when the leaves fall down and birds make a nest
The sun leaves quicker from the sky needing a rest
Spring is when the sun peeks through and flowers burst and bloom
Children zoom with laughter, waiting for the moon
Summer is hot and has very little rain
We go to the beach and wait for the train
I think I feel nervous...

Molly Jones
Warden Hill Primary School, Warden Hill

About Me!

My name is Kacy,
I own pet mice,
And I am nice.
I love sloths,
But not moths.
I like to play,
If my mum says it's okay.
I like Stranger Things,
But nobody sings.
I like going to places,
But I need help with my shoelaces.
I absolutely adore animals,
And some are mammals.
I really don't like snakes,
And some live in lakes.
I love playing games,
And some have names.
My name is Kacy,
And this is me.

Kacy Welch (11)
Widey Court Primary School, Crownhill

The Awesome Me
A kennings poem

Good gamer
Sun lover
Cat lover
Good student
Chocolate liker
Good memory
Dog hater
Decent footballer
Teacher liker
Respectful student
Dogman fan
School lover
Heavy sleeper
Fizzy hater
Maths adorer
Book liker
Juice lover.

Antoni Panasewicz (9)
Worsbrough Common Primary School, Worsbrough Common

This Is Me

I am Amelia
My hair is brown as a door
My eyes are blue as a sky
My smile is as bright as a rainbow
I am fast as a cat
I am as smart as a monkey.

Amelia Rose (8)
Worsbrough Common Primary School, Worsbrough Common

This Is Me!
A kennings poem

Ayan
Football lover
Mancher United fan
FIFA 22 addict
PS4 master
Dog lover
Phone addicter
Laptop addicter
Jolly Rancher gulper
Nakoul.

Ayan Nakoul (8)
Worsbrough Common Primary School, Worsbrough Common

Phoebe's Poem

Phoebe
Friendly, curious
Friend of Amelia
Likes reading and drinking coffee
Feels happy when playing with her sister
Creative, thoughtful
Lunn.

Phoebe Lunn (9)
Worsbrough Common Primary School, Worsbrough Common

All About Me

Libbie
Kind, helpful
Big sister of five and one big brother
Loves drawing, playing with Kane
When I am sad I draw
Playful, cheerful
Storey.

Libbie Storey (9)
Worsbrough Common Primary School, Worsbrough Common

YOUNG WRITERS INFORMATION

We hope you have enjoyed reading this book – and that you will continue to in the coming years.

If you're the parent or family member of an enthusiastic poet or story writer, do visit our website **www.youngwriters.co.uk/subscribe** and sign up to receive news, competitions, writing challenges and tips, activities and much, much more! There's lots to keep budding writers motivated!

If you would like to order further copies of this book, or any of our other titles, then please give us a call or order via your online account.

Young Writers
Remus House
Coltsfoot Drive
Peterborough
PE2 9BF
(01733) 890066
info@youngwriters.co.uk

Join in the conversation!
Tips, news, giveaways and much more!

YoungWritersUK   YoungWritersCW   youngwriterscw